"When you have done the will of God,
you will receive what He has promised."

– Hebrews 10:36 NIV

GW00670233

KNOWING GOD'S UNIQUE PLAN FOR YOUR LIFE

LIFE'S BLUE-PRINT

DEREK PRINCE

LIFE'S BLUEPRINT
Knowing God's Unique Plan for Your Life

© 1986 Derek Prince Ministries–International

This edition DPM-UK 2019. Previously published under the title:
God's Will for Your Life'.

www.dpmuk.org

978-1-78263-663-2	Pub
978-1-78263-664-9	Epub
978-1-78263-665-6	Kindle
Product Code	T096

Derek Prince Ministries · www.derekprince.com
Set in Arno by Raphael Freeman, Renana Typesetting

Contents

1

Jesus, Our Pattern

The subject of this book is related in a very personal and practical way to the life of each one of us – *God's will for your life.*

Let us begin by asking a personal question: do you have a known, clear objective for your life? Or are you drifting through life, being carried here and there by the winds of habit and fashion, tossed by waves of circumstances over which you have no control?

There is nothing more tragic in a human life than aimlessness. If you aim at nothing, you may be sure you will hit it. You may have talent, intelligence, and special abilities, but without an objective your life will end in frustration, because you will have accomplished very little of permanent value.

Herein lies one of the greatest benefits and blessings of the Christian life. As God planned it, the Christian life gives each one of us an objective for living. This objective for living is provided for us by our faith in Christ.

The first picture of the Christian life and its objective that we will look at is found in Hebrews:

> *Therefore, since we are surrounded by such a great cloud of witnesses, let us throw off everything that hinders and the sin that so easily entangles, and let us run with perseverance the race marked out for us. Let us fix our eyes on Jesus, the author and perfecter of our faith, who for the joy set before him endured the cross, scorning its shame, and sat down at the right hand of the throne of God.* Hebrews 12:1–2

There are three important truths mentioned here. First, the Christian life is a race marked out for us in advance. We do not need to mark the course out; that has been done for us. We need only to run the race. However, this race is not a dash or a sprint, but it is much more like a long-distance marathon.

To be able to run this long race, we must throw off everything that hinders us or gets in our way. These things may not always be sinful; nevertheless, they keep us from running the race. For that reason we must eliminate them from our lives.

In this race, there is a particular quality that is emphasized: *perseverance* or *endurance*. For us to finish the race, it will require our perseverance or endurance.

Second, we are to fix our eyes on Jesus. Jesus is our pattern and our inspiration. If we take our eyes off Jesus for any length of time, we will lose our ability to run the race successfully.

Third, Jesus is *the author and perfecter of our faith.* He is the one who set it all in motion. We may recognize that He is the author of our faith, but we often lose sight of the fact that He is also the perfecter. Jesus not only started it, He is going to complete it.

Both in Scripture and in God's dealings in my life, I have seen that He never starts anything He is not capable of finishing. We need to take heart and be encouraged by this fact. Jesus started us off on this race, and He is going to enable us to finish it. He is the author and the perfecter.

Keep these three important things in mind. First, the Christian life is a race in which the course is marked out ahead of us, and it is going to take endurance to complete the race. Second, to be successful we must fix our eyes on Jesus. He is both our pattern and our inspiration. Third, He is both the author and perfecter of our faith. As long as we keep our eyes on Jesus, He will not merely set us going, but He will enable us to keep going and bring us successfully and triumphantly to the finish of the race.

In looking to Jesus as both our pattern and our inspiration in this Christian race, we see that the key to His success was His motivation. Unless we really understand His motivation and enter into it with Him, we will find this race too much for us.

In Hebrews 10:5–10, the writer quotes from Psalm 40 and then applies it to Jesus Christ.

Therefore, when Christ came into the world, he said: "Sacrifice and offering you did not desire, but a body you prepared for me; with burnt offerings and sin offerings you were not pleased. Then I said, 'Here I am – it is written about me in the scroll – I have come to do your will, O God.'" First he said, "Sacrifices and offerings, burnt offerings and sin offerings you did not desire, nor were you pleased with them" (although the law required them to be made). Then he said, "Here I am, I have come to do your will." He sets aside the first to establish the second. And by that will, we have been made holy through the sacrifice of the body of Jesus Christ once for all.　　　Hebrews 10:5–10

Notice the word "*body*" at the beginning. The Lord says, "*Sacrifice and offering you did not desire, but a body you prepared for me.*" At the end the comment is, "*By that will* [the will of God done by Jesus Christ], *we have been made holy through the sacrifice of the body of Jesus Christ once for all.*" God provided Jesus with a body to sacrifice on our behalf. This theme is going to follow all through this study.

5

From this passage we see, first, what Jesus' supreme motivation was: *"I have come to do your will."* That statement was quoted twice for emphasis so it would not be missed. The paramount purpose and single objective of Jesus throughout His earthly life was to do the will of God. He was absolutely clear about it, and He never swerved from it.

Second, in connection with the first, there was a part written for Jesus to play:

"Here I am – it is written about me in the scroll – I have come to do your will, O God." It was written in the scroll of God's Word before He came. Jesus did not write His own part or improvise on the script He was given. He discovered it through studying the Scriptures.

Third, God's will for Jesus culminated in the sacrifice of Jesus' own body. God's purpose and plan in giving Him a body was that Jesus would offer His body as the perfect sacrifice on behalf of mankind.

Note the following three points:

1. Jesus' supreme motivation was to do God's will.

2. There was a part for Him already written in the scroll of Scripture.

3. God's will for Jesus culminated in the sacrifice of His own body.

Each of these three points must have its counterpart in our lives. Every one of those statements that was true about Jesus should be true about us. Each one of us needs the same motivation Jesus had to do God's will and to discover what is written for us in the scroll of Scripture. Finally, the doing of God's will in our lives will culminate in the sacrifice of our own bodies.

2

The Outworking of God's Will

One essential condition for a successful life is to have a clearly defined and steadily pursued objective. Without such an objective a person is like a boat drifting on the open sea, carried here and there by the winds of habit and the waves of circumstance, without any control over his or her own destiny.

As I stated earlier, one of the greatest benefits and blessings of the Christian life is that it provides each one of us with an objective for living. In this respect, Jesus is both our pattern and our inspiration. Let us look at how the commitment to do God's will was practically worked out in the earthly life and ministry of Jesus. We will begin with the well-known incident where Jesus met the woman of Samaria at Jacob's Well. Jesus and His disciples were journeying by foot, back from Judea to Galilee.

They passed through Samaria and came to the place that is still known today as Jacob's Well. Jesus was tired and sat down by the well to rest. Apparently they had run out of food and were hungry, because the disciples had gone into the local town to buy food. Then the woman from Samaria came out to the well, and Jesus had that wonderful conversation with her in which He gave her that beautiful promise about the living water for everyone who was thirsty. The woman became so excited that she left her water pot without collecting water and went back into the town to tell the men about this wonderful person she had met at the well.

As Jesus remained at the well, His disciples came back and found Him sitting there. This is what follows in the account in John's gospel:

Meanwhile his disciples urged him, "Rabbi, eat something." But he said to them, "I have food

to eat that you know nothing about." Then his disciples said to each other, "Could someone have brought him food?" "My food," said Jesus, "is to do the will of him who sent me and to finish his work. Do you not say, 'Four months more and then the harvest'? I tell you, open your eyes and look at the fields! They are ripe for harvest. Even now the reaper draws his wages, even now he harvests the crop for eternal life, so that the sower and the reaper may be glad together."
John 4:31–36

Here is the clear statement of Jesus: *"My food...is to do the will of him who sent me."* The central motivation of His entire earthly life was always to do the will of the One who sent Him. There are two results of this motivation in the life of Jesus that should have their counterpart in our lives.

First, Jesus' commitment to do the will of God actually worked supernatural, physical restoration in Him. When He came to the well, He was tired and hungry. Jesus sat down, but instead of eating, He flowed in the will of God in His conversation with this needy woman. In putting

God's will above His own physical needs, He received supernatural restoration. When the disciples came with food, Jesus was not particularly interested. He said, "I have already eaten." His disciples could not understand what kind of food He could have had. Jesus explained, *"My food ... is to do the will of him who sent me and to finish his work."* Food is the thing that gives us physical strength and sustains us. Jesus said, "That is what sustains Me and keeps me going – My commitment to do the will of the One who sent Me."

Second, Jesus had a different viewpoint. He began to speak about how to look at the world. He said, "You look at the world one way; I look at the world another. You say there are four more months to harvest, but for Me the harvest field is already ripe. I am already reaping." Jesus was referring to His encounter with the Samaritan woman. He was reaping the harvest in that village at that very moment. A few minutes later, the woman came back with all the men in the village, and Jesus shared with them.

The disciples looked at things from a purely natural point of view. They said, "It is not yet time for harvest." In contrast, Jesus had a spiritual viewpoint. He saw things from another perspective. Jesus' commitment to do the will of God was what gave Him this spiritual insight.

Approximately two-thirds of the way through the next chapter of John's gospel, we find another statement Jesus made that has much to teach us about the result of being committed to doing God's will. Jesus is discussing the healing of a man who had been paralyzed for many years. In the middle of this discussion, Jesus makes this statement:

> *"I can do nothing on My own initiative. As I hear, I judge; and My judgment is just, because I do not seek My own will, but the will of Him who sent Me."*   John 5:30 NASB

Notice Jesus' words, *"My judgment is just."* In other words, Jesus was saying, *"My judgment is right."* Why? *"Because I do not seek My own will, but the will of Him who sent Me."* Here we find a third result of that commitment to do the will of God. I would call it "just judgment" or "impartial discernment."

Jesus was never fooled. Nobody ever

deceived Him. Jesus discerned the truth in everyone who came to Him. He saw into their inner motives and knew what they were really after. Jesus knew how to reach and touch them where they needed to be touched, whether it was spiritually or physically, because of His commitment to doing God's will.

How can we avoid foolish judgment and wrong appraisals of people and situations? We find the key in John 5:30, where Jesus said, "My judgment is just; My discernment is accurate. I see things the way they really are." Why? *"Because I do not seek My own will, but the will of Him who sent Me."*

Jesus' judgment was not clouded by His desire to get His own way. He was in neutral, so to speak, until the Father moved Him. Jesus waited for the Father's revelation of His will, and then Jesus made a just and accurate judgment.

3
Further Outworking of God's Will

So far, we have looked at the way in which Jesus' commitment to do God's will was practically worked out in His earthly life and ministry. I pointed out three specific results in His life. First, there was physical restoration. At Jacob's Well He was tired and hungry, yet in doing the will of God by sharing the truth with that Samaritan woman, Jesus received physical restoration. He was no longer hungry when His disciples returned with food.

Second, there was a proper view of the situation. Jesus saw the harvest field with the eyes of God, while His disciples still looked with natural eyes. Jesus' commitment to do the will of God gave Him a view that differed from the perspectives of those around Him.

Third, there was just judgment or impartial discernment. Jesus said, *"My judgment is just, because I do not seek My own will, but the will of Him who sent Me"* (John 5:30 NASB). He was never fooled or carried away by His own wishful thinking, emotions, or reactions. Jesus always waited for the Father's revelation concerning every situation.

Let us continue by looking at two further results of Jesus' commitment to do the will of God. We are going to look at the discourse of Jesus after He fed the five thousand with five loaves and two fishes, and specifically at the spiritual application to Himself.

> *Then Jesus declared, "I am the bread of life. He who comes to me will never go hungry, and he who believes in me will never be thirsty. But as I told you, you have seen me and still you do not believe. All that the Father gives me will come to me, and whoever comes to me I will never drive away. For I have come down from heaven not to*

do my will but to do the will of him who sent me. [It is significant that there must be a setting aside of our own will before we can do the will of God.] *And this is the will of him who sent me, that I shall lose none of all that he has given me, but raise them up at the last day. For my Father's will is that everyone who looks to the Son and believes in him shall have eternal life, and I will raise him up at the last day."*

John 6:35–40

Jesus had set aside His own will and, at the end of His discourse, He referred to *"my Father's will."* I never read that statement, *"I am the bread of life,"* without being moved. *"Everyone who looks to* [Me] *and believes in* [Me] *shall have eternal life and I will raise him up at the last day."* What a beautiful offer from the One who can feed and give life to a hungry, dying world!

But what was the price Jesus had to pay? It was, "Not doing My will, but the will of Him who sent Me." As long as we are busy with our own plans, purposes, and objectives, we cannot be channels of divine life. Since this was true even of Jesus, how much more so is it for you and me? If we want the privilege of being God's bread, broken to feed a hungry world, then we must make a renunciation. "*Not…my will but… the will of him who sent me.*"

This was Paul's personal testimony, in his second letter to the Corinthians:

> *We always carry around in our body the death of Jesus, so that the life of Jesus may also be revealed in our body. For we who are alive are always being given over to death for Jesus' sake, so that his life may be revealed in our mortal body. So then, death is at work in us, but life is at work in you.*   2 Corinthians 4:10–12

Paul explained, "*So then, death is at work in us, but life is at work in you.*" The world needs channels of life, but there is a price to pay. If you want to be a channel of life to others, death has first to work in you. We cannot have it any other way or change the order.

The pattern is clear: when death is at work in you, then life is at work in others. You are here not to do your own will, but the will of Him who sent you. The will of Him who sent you is to feed and give life to a hungry and dying world. If you will renounce your own will and pursue with single-hearted devotion the will of God as revealed for your life, then you, too, in your own measure, can be food for a hungry world and life to a dying world. However, this is not possible while you are concerned with doing your own will.

There was one more result produced in the life of Jesus by His commitment to do the will of the Father. We can discover it in Jesus' great high-priestly prayer to the Father on behalf of His disciples before He was separated from them. This beautiful expression of Christ is found in the latter part of the gospel of John:

> *I glorified Thee on the earth, having accomplished the work which Thou hast given Me to do.* John 17:4 NASB

Where this version says, "*accomplished,*" it is a translation of a form of the Greek word, *teleios,* which also means "*to finish*" or "*to complete.*" "*I glorified Thee on the earth, having* [finished] *the work which Thou hast given Me to do.*" Throughout the Gospels, the emphasis of Jesus was not merely on doing the will of God, but on finishing the work. In connection with the incident of the Samaritan woman at Jacob's Well, He had said, *"My food is to do the will of Him who sent Me, and to finish His work"* (John 4:34 NKJV).

Jesus was always looking ahead to the triumphant conclusion of His task. Here He says, "Now I have brought glory to You, O Father, on the earth, because I have come to the end of the work. I have finished it." Returning to the picture of a race we considered previously, we could say that Jesus is finishing the race. He is just about to breast the tape, and, in doing that, He says, "I have brought glory to God."

Doing the will of God will always bring glory to Him. Whatever task God calls you to do, if you do it thoroughly and finish it, you can bring glory to Him. The task God assigns to you may be simple, humble, or ordinary. It may entail being the best wife and mother, a godly husband and father, an efficient secretary, or a good businessman. Whatever the task, if you finish it and do a thorough job, you will bring glory to God.

Self-seeking, half-hearted service never glorifies God. One of the reasons it does not is because such a person's motive for serving is always wrapped up in himself or herself. There are Christians, even ministers, who are concerned for their own glory rather than God's glory. They may attract large followings and get people interested in their gifts and ministries, but the ultimate end will not be the glory of God.

In order to glorify God, we must have a single vision for the task God has assigned us. In addition, we need to have a fixed determination that we will finish the task no matter what it costs. There is nothing I desire more than to come to the end of my ministry and life here on Earth and be able to say in my own limited measure, "*I glorified Thee on the earth, having accomplished the work which Thou hast given me to do.*"

4
The Culmination: The Cross

We have been taking Jesus as both the pattern and the inspiration for living. We have seen that the supreme motivation of His life was to do God's will as revealed in the scroll of Scripture. Our key verse is this:

> Then [Jesus] said, "Here I am – it is written about me in the scroll – I have come to do your will, O God."　　　　Hebrews 10:7

Two vital points are evident: first, the motive for which Jesus came was to do God's will; second, the part He had to play was already written in the scroll. That should also be true of you and me.

We have also looked at five specific results in the earthly life of Jesus that came through His commitment to do the will of God:

1. He received physical restoration in a supernatural way.
2. He had a proper view of the situation He was in, different from that of the people around Him.
3. He rendered just judgment or impartial discernment. (Jesus was never gullible or deceived. He always saw exactly how a thing really was.)
4. He was a channel of life to a dying world.
5. He glorified God on the earth.

As He attained all these results, Jesus set the pattern for us to follow.

Let us continue by looking at the culmination of God's will in the life of Jesus. In the tenth chapter of Hebrews, we discover that God's supreme will for Jesus was the sacrifice of His body:

Therefore, when Christ came into the world, he said: "Sacrifice and offering you did not desire, but a body you prepared for me; with burnt offerings and sin offerings you were not pleased. Then I said, 'Here I am – it is written about me in the scroll – I have come to do your will, O God.'" First he said, "Sacrifices and offerings, burnt offerings and sin offerings you did not desire, nor were you pleased with them" (although the law required them to be made). Then he said, "Here I am, I have come to do your will." He sets aside the first to establish the second. And by that will, we have been made holy through the sacrifice of the body of Jesus Christ once for all. Hebrews 10:5–10

Jesus came to this world to do the will of His Father. In order to do God's will, God prepared a body for Him. The outworking of that will demanded that Jesus sacrifice His own body. The culmination or ultimate goal of the life of Jesus was to sacrifice His body on behalf of the world.

As we have seen, there was a continual emphasis in the mind of Jesus, not merely to do God's work, but to finish it and complete God's will. The nearer Jesus came to the end of His earthly ministry, the stronger this emphasis became in His life.

Let us look at a statement in the gospel of Luke:

> *And it came about, when the days were approaching for His ascension* [literally, "His 'taking up,'" which refers to Jesus being taken up through His death on the cross], *that He resolutely set His face to go to Jerusalem.*
>
> Luke 9:51 NASB

Notice that key phrase, "He resolutely set His face." Jesus knew what lay ahead of Him. He had already told His disciples, although they refused to believe Him. As the time of completion approached, *"He resolutely set His face."* He was determined to finish His work.

The prophet Isaiah, by the Spirit of Christ, prophetically foretold the culmination of the life of Jesus on earth, as follows:

> *The Sovereign LORD has given me an instructed tongue,* [a disciple's tongue – Jesus was the

disciple of the Father], *to know the word that sustains the weary. He wakens me morning by morning, wakens my ear to listen like one being taught.* Isaiah 50:4

Jesus was always in the school of discipleship with the Father. At the beginning of each day, as Jesus spent time in prayer, He received His directions for that day when He heard the Father's voice speak to Him.

Continuing in Isaiah, we read:

The Sovereign LORD has opened my ears, and I have not been rebellious; I have not drawn back. I offered my back to those who beat me, my cheeks to those who pulled out my beard; I did not hide my face from mocking and spitting. Isaiah 50:5–6

It is very important to see that Jesus gave His back to those who beat Him. He freely gave it because it was the Father's will and direction. He heard the Father tell Him, "That's what I sent you to do, My Son," and so He did not withhold Himself. He gave Himself over to His torturers. Finishing the passage in Isaiah, we find:

Because the Sovereign LORD helps me, I will not be disgraced. Therefore have I set my face like flint, and I know I will not be put to shame.

Isaiah 50:7

Luke said, *"He resolutely set His face."* Prophetically writing 700 years earlier, Isaiah said, *"Therefore have I set my face like flint."* Jesus knew what He was going to endure. In fact, it is written in the previous verses of Isaiah, *"I offered my back to those who beat me, my cheeks to those who pulled out my beard; I did not hide my face from mocking and spitting."*

In effect Jesus said in His heart, "I have set My face like a flint. No matter what lies ahead, I'm going to go through with it because My purpose is to do the work that God has assigned to Me and to finish it." Now we come to the actual culmination of the earthly life of Jesus. Jesus had been on the cross for three hours or more, and He was nearing His end. We read in the gospel of John:

Later, knowing that all was now completed, and so that the Scripture would be fulfilled, Jesus

said, "I am thirsty." A jar of wine vinegar was
there, so they soaked a sponge in it, put the
sponge on a stalk of the hyssop plant, and lifted
it to Jesus' lips. When he had received the drink,
Jesus said, "It is finished." With that, he bowed
his head and gave up his spirit.

John 19:28–30

Jesus released His own spirit to the Father
(Luke 23:46). He had told His disciples earlier,

"Therefore My Father loves Me, because I lay
down My life that I may take it again. No one
takes it from Me, but I lay it down of Myself. I
have power to lay it down, and I have power
to take it again. This command I have received
from My Father. John 10:17–28 NKJV

Before Jesus dismissed His spirit, one of His
last great utterances was, *"It is finished"* (John
19:30). What was finished? He had finished the
task of His earthly assignment. Throughout
His life He had been saying, *"My food…is to*
do the will of him who sent me and to finish his
work" (John 4:34). Then, in anticipation of this

29

moment, in His prayer, which is found in the seventeenth chapter of John, He expressed, "I have glorified You on Earth. I have finished the work You gave Me to do." On the cross it was actually fulfilled as He cried out, "*It is finished.*"

That was not a cry of defeat. That was a cry of triumph! "'*It is finished*!' Everything that was assigned to Me I have done. I have done it completely. I have left nothing out. Now redemption is available through My sacrifice there on the cross!"

In Greek, "*It is finished*!" is just one word: *tetelestai*. It is the perfect tense of a verb that means "to complete something," "to finish something," "to do something perfectly." In searching for a way to communicate it in English, I thought of such phrases as these: "It is completely complete," "It is perfectly perfect," and "Everything that had to be done (for man's redemption through the sacrifice of My body) has been done."

Jesus would not release His spirit until He could say, "*It is finished,*" and until He knew that He had done everything required of Him by the Father. That was the goal toward which His life was directed. That was the supreme motivation that had caused Him to set His face like a flint and had enabled Him to go through the shame, pain, rejection, and disgrace.

I have often heard it said that it was not the nails that held Jesus to the cross, but rather it was His commitment to the Father's will. That commitment was something from which He would not swerve or turn to the right or to the left. To do His Father's will no matter what was Jesus' motivation. That was His purpose in living here on Earth. God had given Jesus a body. He knew from the Scriptures that God's purpose for His body was that He should sacrifice it on the cross on behalf of mankind. Everything Jesus did was directed to the fulfillment of the will of God and the completion of His assignment.

5
Following the Example of Jesus

We have been consistently looking to Jesus as both our pattern and our inspiration. We have seen that the commitment to do God's will was the motivation that brought Jesus down from heaven to Earth. This commitment shaped and directed the entire course of His earthly life and ministry and culminated in the sacrifice of His own body on the cross.

Let us consider how we can apply this example of Jesus to our own lives. Three main steps are necessary in applying the pattern Jesus gave us. The first step is to will to do God's will. The apostle John recorded that Jesus said:

If anyone chooses to do God's will, he will find out whether my teaching comes from God or whether I speak on my own.　　John 7:17

The Greek word that is translated here as "*chooses*" is actually a form of the verb, *thelo*, which means "to will" or "to determine." If anyone chooses to do God's will or if anybody wills to do God's will, he or she will find out whether Jesus speaks on His own.

Many religious people underestimate the function of the will in their spiritual lives. Many people's lives are directed by impressions, feelings, and promptings. However, the thing that ultimately determines the direction of our lives is the exercise of our will. That is the decisive factor. We cannot lead a right life if we do not will to lead a right life.

Jesus sets before us this challenge, which is also an invitation: will you set your will to do God's will? Without meeting that challenge, leading a right life will never happen. It does not come about by inspiration, wonderful preaching, or somebody praying for us.

There must come a point in our lives where

we make a personal decision. *Decision* is a key word. We have to decide: "I am going to do God's will." Jesus told us, *"If anyone chooses to do God's will,* [then] *he will find out whether my teaching comes from God."*

It is important to understand that we do not find out first, and then will to do God's will; we first choose to do, and then we find out. Many people have the order wrong. They pray, "God, show me the whole thing. I want to understand it all first, and then I will decide to do what You tell me." However, that is not how it works. God does not scratch an itching intellect. If you just want to know out of your intellectual curiosity without the willingness to make a commitment, God will not reveal His will to you. But, if you will to do God's will, then understanding, insight, and revelation will follow.

Let me put it another way: commitment leads to understanding, not understanding to commitment. You do not first understand God's will and then commit yourself to do it. You commit yourself to do God's will; then, to your committed mind, God begins to unfold His will. All of us come to a point in our lives where we must make a vital decision for ourselves: "My decision is to do God's will." We cannot say "if" or "perhaps." That is not a commitment.

The second step is the sacrifice of our bodies. The doing of God's will culminated for Jesus in the sacrifice of His body. He knew that when He set out to do God's will. It may surprise you to know – but it is very clearly stated in Scripture – that for you and me to do God's will requires, likewise, the sacrifice of our bodies. However, there is a difference. The sacrifice of the body of Jesus meant its death. We are told by Paul to sacrifice our *living* bodies:

> *Therefore, I urge you, brothers, in view of God's mercy, to offer your bodies as living sacrifices, holy and pleasing to God – which is your spiritual act of worship.*   Romans 12:1

In essence, God says to each of us, "In the light of all that I have done for you, the response I require is for you to offer your body to Me as a living sacrifice. Place your body on My altar. Make your body available to Me without reservation."

If you offer your body as a living sacrifice to God, you no longer claim ownership of your body. You no longer decide where your body will go or what your body will do, eat, or wear. You have given up the right to make those decisions. From now on, your body belongs to God. You have sacrificed it to Him, a living body, on His altar.

Whatever is placed on the altar of God belongs thereafter to God. It no longer belongs to the person who gave it. God requires that we, just like Jesus, sacrifice our bodies. The difference is that Jesus sacrificed His body through death, but we are asked to sacrifice our bodies while they are still alive. We are to hand our bodies over to God and give up our rights and our claims to them.

That may sound very frightening, but I want to tell you that it is very exciting. Somehow, we picture that what this means is that we will end up in some lonely wasteland, wearing rags and living on bread and water, but that is not what God has in mind.

"For I know the plans that I have for you," declares the LORD, "plans for welfare and not

for calamity to give you a future and a hope."
Jeremiah 29:11 NASB

God has all sorts of ideas about what He might do with you and your body, but He is not going to tell you until your body belongs to Him. You must commit it to Him first; then you will be given understanding.

After offering our bodies as living sacrifices, we come to the next step, which is renewing the mind. Paul described this very clearly in Romans:

> *Do not conform any longer to the pattern of this world, but be transformed by the renewing of your mind. Then you will be able to test and approve what God's will is – his good, pleasing and perfect will.* Romans 12:2

Once you have taken the decisive step of handing your body over to God as a living sacrifice, something happens in your mind. That decision releases something in your mind, and it becomes renewed. You no longer think the way the world thinks. Worldly people are self-centered in their thinking. "If I do this, how will it affect me? If I say this, will I get a raise? Will I be promoted? Will people like me?" It all centers around "me." But, the renewed mind centers around God. "Will this glorify God? Is this God's purpose in my life?"

"With the mind thus renewed," Paul explained to us, "then you can find out the will of God." God will not give that revelation until you have made the commitment. The commitment leads to the renewing of your mind. With your mind renewed you can discern the will of God and find the path God has for you in life.

In most cases God's path for you will be very different from what you think it might be. The Devil will be right there on your shoulder, whispering in your ear that God's way is going to be miserable and hard. Satan will tell you that you are going to spend the rest of your life washing dishes or living somewhere in a desert. That could be true but, most probably, it will not be that way. However, you will never know until you make the commitment.

The outworking of this surrender of your body to God will be the same as it was in the life of Jesus. There were five results of this determination in the life of Jesus, and you can anticipate the same results in your life when you surrender your body and your will to God.

1. There was supernatural, physical restoration. Jesus was not limited to His own physical strength, nor will you be if you are committed to the will of God.

2. There was proper vision. Jesus saw things the way God sees things, and so will you when you are committed to the will of God.

3. There was just judgment or clear discernment. Jesus was not fooled, and He was not deceived. He saw things in people the way they really were.

4. Jesus became a channel of life to a dying world. Likewise, you and I can be channels of life when we are committed to doing God's will.

5. Jesus said, "*I have glorified You on the earth. I have finished the work which You have given Me to do*" (John 17:4 NKJV). If we will commit ourselves to God and His will and to finishing it with all our hearts, we, too, will be able to glorify God on the earth.

When you totally surrender your body and your will to God, yielding any further claim of self-control to Him, you will glorify the Lord and find deep peace and personal satisfaction in your soul. You will discover a new sense of purpose as God reveals His will for your life.

About the Author

Derek Prince (1915–2003) was born in India of British parents. He was educated as a scholar of Greek and Latin at Eton College and King's College, Cambridge in England. Upon graduation he held a fellowship (equivalent to a professorship) in Ancient and Modern Philosophy at King's College. Prince also studied Hebrew, Aramaic, and modern languages at Cambridge and the Hebrew University in Jerusalem. As a student, he was a philosopher and self-proclaimed agnostic.

Bible Teacher

While in the British Medical Corps during World War II, Prince began to study the Bible as a philosophical work. Converted through a powerful encounter with Jesus Christ, he was baptized in the Holy Spirit a few days later. Out of this encounter, he formed two conclusions: first, that Jesus Christ is alive; second, that the Bible is a true, relevant, up-to-date book. These conclusions altered the whole course of his life, which he then devoted to studying and teaching the Bible as the Word of God.

Discharged from the army in Jerusalem in 1945, he married Lydia Christensen, founder of a children's home there. Upon their marriage, he immediately became father to Lydia's eight adopted daughters – six Jewish, one Palestinian Arab, and one English. Together, the family saw the rebirth of the state of Israel in 1948. In the late 1950s, they adopted another daughter while Prince was serving as principal of a teacher training college in Kenya.

In 1963, the Princes immigrated to the United States and pastored a church in Seattle. In 1973, Prince became one of the founders of Intercessors for America. His book Shaping History through Prayer and Fasting has awakened Christians around the world to their responsibility to pray for their governments. Many consider underground translations of the book as instrumental in the fall of communist regimes in the USSR, East Germany, and Czechoslovakia.

Lydia Prince died in 1975, and Prince married Ruth Baker (a single mother to three adopted children) in 1978. He met his second wife, like his first wife, while she was serving the Lord in Jerusalem. Ruth died in December 1998 in Jerusalem, where they had lived since 1981.

Teaching, Preaching and Broadcasting

Until a few years before his own death in 2003 at the age of eighty-eight, Prince persisted in the ministry God had called him to as he traveled the world, imparting God's revealed truth, praying for the sick and afflicted, and sharing his prophetic insights into world events in the light of Scripture. Internationally recognized as a Bible scholar and spiritual patriarch, Derek Prince established a teaching ministry that spanned six continents and more than sixty years.

He is the author of more than fifty books, six hundred audio teachings, and one hundred video teachings, many of which have been translated and published in more than one hundred languages.

He pioneered teaching on such groundbreaking themes as generational curses, the biblical significance of Israel, and demonology. Prince's radio program, which began in 1979, has been translated into more than a dozen languages and continues to touch lives. Derek's main gift of explaining the Bible and its teaching in a clear and simple way has helped build a foundation of faith in millions of lives. His nondenominational, nonsectarian approach has made his teaching equally relevant and helpful to people from all racial and religious backgrounds, and his teaching is estimated to have reached more than half the globe.

DPM Worldwide Ministry

In 2002, he said, "It is my desire – and I believe the Lord's desire – that this ministry continue the work, which God began through me over sixty years ago, until Jesus returns." Derek Prince Ministries International continues to reach out to believers in over 140 countries with Derek's teaching, fulfilling the mandate to keep on "until

Jesus returns." This is accomplished through the outreaches of more than thirty Derek Prince offices around the world, including primary work in Australia, Canada, China, France, Germany, the Netherlands, New Zealand, Norway, Russia, South Africa, Switzerland, the United Kingdom, and the United States. For current information about these and other worldwide locations, visit www.derekprince.com.

Inspired by Derek's teaching?
Help make it available to others!

If you have been inspired and blessed by this Derek Prince resource you can help make it available to a spiritually hungry believer in other countries, such as China, the Middle East, India, Africa or Russia.

Even a small gift from you will ensure that that a pastor, Bible college student or a believer elsewhere in the world receives a free copy of a Derek Prince resource in their own language.

Donate now: www.dpmuk.org/give

RECEIVING GOD'S PROMISES

Every day, we face challenges that can be met through God's powerful provision. In a very practical way, renowned Bible teacher Derek Prince shows you how to address your difficulties and have your needs supplied by applying the specific promises appropriate for each situation. Journal edition.

£9.99
ISBN 978-1-78263-607-6
Paperback and eBook

Derek Prince Ministries Offices Worldwide

DPM – Asia/Pacific
38 Hawdon Street
Sydenham
Christchurch 8023
New Zealand
T: + 64 3 366 4443
E: admin@dpm.co.nz
W: www.dpm.co.nz and www.derekprince.in

DPM – Australia
15 Park Road
Seven Hills
New South Wales 2147
Australia
T: +61 2 9838 7778
E: enquiries@au.derekprince.com
W: www.derekprince.com.au

DPM – Canada
P.O. Box 8354 Halifax
Nova Scotia B3K 5M1
Canada
T: + 1 902 443 9577
E: enquiries.dpm@eastlink.ca
W: www.derekprince.org

DPM – France
B.P. 31, Route d'Oupia
34210 Olonzac
France
T: + 33 468 913872
E: info@derekprince.fr
W: www.derekprince.fr

DPM – Germany
Söldenhofstr. 10
83308 Trostberg
Germany
T: + 49 8621 64146
E: ibl@ibl-dpm.net
W: www.ibl-dpm.net

DPM – Netherlands

Nijverheidsweg 12

7005 BJ Doetinchem

Netherlands

T: +31 251–255044

E: info@derekprince.nl

W: www.derekprince.nl

DPM – Norway

P.O. Box 129

Lodderfjord

N-5881 Bergen

Norway

T: +47 928 39855

E: sverre@derekprince.no

W: www.derekprince.no

Derek Prince Publications Pte. Ltd.

P.O. Box 2046

Robinson Road Post Office

Singapore 904046

T: + 65 6392 1812

E: dpmchina@singnet.com.sg

W: www.dpmchina.org (English)

www.ygmweb.org (Chinese)

DPM – South Africa
P.O. Box 33367
Glenstantia
0010 Pretoria
South Africa
T: +27 12 348 9537
E: enquiries@derekprince.co.za
W: www.derekprince.co.za

DPM – Switzerland
Alpenblick 8
CH-8934 Knonau
Switzerland
T: + 41 44 768 25 06
E: dpm-ch@ibl-dpm.net
W: www.ibl-dpm.net

DPM – UK
PO Box 393
Hitchin SG5 9EU
United Kingdom
T: + 44 1462 492100
E: enquiries@dpmuk.org
W: www.dpmuk.org

DPM – USA
P.O. Box 19501
Charlotte NC 28219
USA
T: + 1 704 357 3556
E: ContactUs@derekprince.org
W: www.derekprince.org